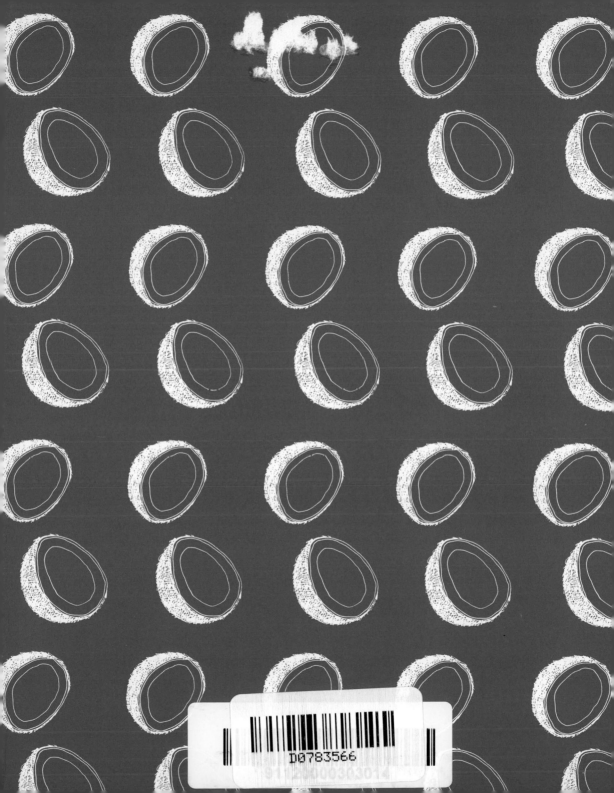

COCONUT

THE GOODNESS OF
COCONUT

40 IRRESISTIBLE ENERGY-PACKED RECIPES

EMILY JONZEN

PHOTOGRAPHY BY CLARE WINFIELD

KYLE BOOKS

CONTENTS

COCONUT IS GREAT

The term 'superfood' has been bandied around a lot in recent years, referring to numerous ingredients that some home cooks will never have heard of. New scientific research instructing us what to eat and what to avoid can be nothing short of confusing.

The myriad health benefits of the humble coconut, however, cement it as a superfood that is here to stay. Coconut, in its many forms, has been proven to be rich in vitamins B, C and E, as well as the minerals selenium, iron, calcium, magnesium and phosphorous. Coconut milk is a great alternative for those with dairy intolerances, while coconut water is so high in phosphates and natural electrolytes that it has become the recovery drink of choice for athletes. Coconut flour is also a great source of fibre and protein. Far from an inferior substitute to dairy and gluten, coconut packs in delicious flavour, with added nutritional punch.

THE BENEFITS
OF COCONUT

Infinitely versatile, coconut can be used in simple, everyday recipes to delicious effect. This book is divided into four chapters by ingredient. The Milk & Water chapter provides easy recipes for smoothies and juices, soups and curries, while the Oil section focuses on everyday meals, from granola to risotto. The Flour chapter offers recipes for delicious cakes, pancakes and bread and the Desiccated section shows you how to enhance dishes with the earthy nuttiness of coconut.

BUYING
THE BEST

Coconut products may be more expensive than their mainstream alternatives, but a little goes a long way, so buy the best you can (see pages 10–11).

Top tips for buying good coconut

♦ When buying a fresh, whole coconut, check for ripeness by shaking it to make sure that there is still plenty of water inside – a dry coconut will be overripe and soapy-tasting.

♦ Check that there are no cracks in the skin and the dark brown 'eyes' at either end are intact and dry.

How to open a coconut

To open a coconut, place it on a sturdy chopping board with the 'eyes' facing up. Determine the softest eye by holding a screwdriver or skewer to each eye and seeing which pierces most easily. Pierce the eye, then drain the juice into a jug.

Now turn the coconut on its side and use the blunt edge of a heavy knife to repeatedly tap around the circumference of the coconut until it begins to split.

Continue until you have two equal parts. The flesh can now be eased away from the shell with a spoon.

How to store a coconut

A whole coconut can be refrigerated for up to two months. Once opened, the flesh can be kept in the fridge for up to 3 days, covered. Alternatively, the flesh can be grated and frozen for up to six months.

SOURCING

Purchasing coconut in its many forms can be a little pricey so it's important to make sure that you get the best value for money.

Water

Found inside the coconut, it's sweetness differs depending on age and environment. High in electrolytes, fibre, potassium, magnesium and phosphorous, it is ideal to drink after exercise. Because of its balanced sugar levels and vitamin and mineral richness, it is far healthier than high sugar fruit juices. While the water can be enjoyed alone or in drinks, its not economical to regularly drain coconuts. Happily, it is readily available in cartons. Try to buy unsweetened, and organic, for purity. Once opened, refrigerate and use within three days.

Milk & Cream

Made from grated coconut flesh soaked in hot water. Cream rises to the surface and is skimmed off, then the remaining liquid and flesh are squeezed through a cheesecloth to extract the thick milk. A great alternative to dairy as it is lactose-free, hormone-free and rich in B vitamins, iron and copper.

Coconut milk and cream also come in cans and cartons and can be found in most supermarkets. If you are concerned about the fat content, opt for whole fat coconut milk and halve the quantity; reduced-fat milk has been watered down. Keep unused milk or cream in an airtight container and refrigerate for up to three days.

Flour

Made from dehydrated, ground coconut flesh. It is gluten-free, has almost double the fibre of wheat bran, and is far richer in protein than wheat, rye or cornflour. It is very light, making it useful in cakes, muffins and pancakes, but it may need to be mixed with xanthum gum to mimic the stretchy gluten proteins that hold wheat flour products together. It is very absorbent and swells upon contact with liquid, so ratios to egg and other liquids are different to wheat flour.

Coconut flour is available in large supermarkets, health food shops and online. Try to buy organic; it is fairly expensive, but you use far less of it than conventional flour – often 2–3 tablespoons instead of 100g. Once opened, keep in an airtight container in a cool, dark place until the expiry date.

Dried and Desiccated

Made by cutting or grating the flesh, blanching it to remove impurities and then drying until the moisture level reaches 3 per cent (from 19 per cent). Try to buy organic, and sprinkle it over smoothies, fruit, granola and yogurt, as well as curries, chicken and other savoury dishes. It is delicious raw or lightly toasted and will keep in an airtight container for several months.

Sugar

Boiled and dehydrated sap of the coconut palm flower., it can be used in place of cane sugar, though it is richer in taste and lighter in weight, so don't substitute it measure for measure. It has a fairly low glycaemic index, which makes it a popular substitute for diabetics. Some manufacturers mix it with cane sugar, so check the label to ensure it is pure.

Oil

Coconut oil can be swapped for olive and sunflower oils in most cooking. It is great for sautéing and gentle frying, but its relatively low smoke point (due to it being unrefined) means it is not suitable for deep frying or cooking at very high temperatures. It has a mildly sweet, nutty taste that complements lots of foods. You can buy unflavoured oil, but it will be more processed and less nutritious.

Whilst coconut oil is high in saturated fat, it is beneficial for the heart due to the high percentage of lauric acid, which prevents high blood pressure and lowers cholesterol. Its antifungal, antibacterial and antiviral properties are also believed to strengthen the immune system.

The myriad health benefits of coconut oil will be most potent in unrefined, organic, virgin and raw coconut oil, free of the preserving chemicals that may be found in cheaper, refined coconut oil. Good-quality coconut oil is now available in most supermarkets as well as health food shops. The oil is solid at room temperature and will need to be melted over a low heat as necessary. Store in the jar with the lid firmly sealed and away from direct sunlight.

MILK
& WATER

COCONUT & ALMOND
GREEN SMOOTHIE

*VEGETARIAN *DAIRY-FREE *GLUTEN-FREE

The creamy nut butter and sweet coconut water counterbalance any bitterness from the greens in this refreshing smoothie – a perfectly nutritious start to the day.

Serves 2

2 bananas, roughly
   chopped and frozen
2 tablespoons nut butter
2 large handfuls of
   spinach
500ml coconut water
Ice cubes

1. Place the ingredients in a blender and whizz until smooth. Serve immediately or pour into a portable cup to drink on the go.

ORANGE, GINGER
& COCONUT JUICE

*VEGETARIAN *DAIRY-FREE *GLUTEN-FREE

This warming, spicy drink is ideal for fighting off winter colds and flu. Coconut water is anti-bacterial and anti-fungal, whilst the ginger is also anti-viral.

Serves 2

2 oranges, peeled
4cm piece of fresh ginger,
   peeled
500ml coconut water
Crushed ice, to serve

1. Feed the ingredients through a juicer and serve immediately over crushed ice. If you don't have juicer, simply squeeze the orange into a jug and finely grate in the ginger. Add the coconut water, stir and pour over ice.

CARDAMOM HOT CHOCOLATE

*VEGETARIAN *GLUTEN-FREE

The creaminess of coconut milk makes it ideal for a luxurious hot chocolate, plus it has more iron and copper than cow's milk, to help keep your immune system healthy. Cosy up with this decadent, aromatic treat.

Serves 2

250ml coconut milk
250ml boiling water
2 green cardamom pods,
   split with the back of a knife
100g good-quality dark
   chocolate, minimum
   70 per cent cocoa solids,
   finely chopped
Sea salt
Maple syrup

1. Heat the milk in a small saucepan with the water and the cardamom over a low heat until starting to simmer. Remove from the heat and stir through the chocolate until it has melted.

2. To serve, add a pinch of salt and maple syrup to taste, and reheat if necessary, but without boiling. Pour into individual mugs.

This goes really well with the Oat & Sour Cherry Cookies on page 87.

COCONUT & BERRY BIRCHER MUESLI

*VEGETARIAN *DAIRY-FREE

This twist on a Swiss staple soaks overnight in coconut milk and apple juice to be enjoyed with berries and apple the next morning. I've suggested topping the muesli with raspberries, but any fruit works well.

Serves 2

50g rolled oats
150ml coconut milk
100ml apple juice (not
  from concentrate)

To serve
30g whole almonds,
  roughly chopped
1 dessert apple, roughly
  grated
150g fresh or frozen
  raspberries
Maple syrup (optional)

1. Place the oats in a bowl or measuring jug and pour over the coconut milk and apple juice. Cover and refrigerate for a minimum of 2 hours or, preferably, overnight.

2. To serve, spoon the muesli into two bowls and loosen with a little extra juice if necessary. Scatter over the almonds, apple and raspberries and serve with a drizzle of maple syrup (optional).

BANANA & BERRY SMOOTHIE BOWL

*VEGETARIAN *DAIRY-FREE *GLUTEN-FREE

Start the day with a bright and colourful smoothie bowl. It's a delicious way to pack in lots of nutrients first thing in the morning.

Serves 2

2 bananas, 1 roughly
   chopped and frozen, 1 whole
200ml coconut milk
1 dessert apple, roughly
   chopped
2 tablespoons chia seeds
400g mixed berries (e.g.
   blueberries, raspberries
   and strawberries)
Filtered or spring water

To serve
2 tablespoons mixed seeds
2 tablespoons coconut chips

1. Place the frozen banana, coconut milk, apple and chia seeds in a blender or food-processor. Tip in the berries, saving a few for decoration. Blend the mixture until smooth, adding a little water if it is too thick.

2. Divide the smoothie between two bowls and scatter over the remaining berries, mixed seeds and coconut chips. Slice the remaining banana and arrange around the other toppings before serving.

Opt for frozen berries
if fresh are out of
season – they're much
cheaper and will
give the smoothie a
thicker, slightly creamy
consistency.

PRAWN TACOS WITH COCONUT & LIME

*DAIRY-FREE

These light and flavoursome tacos are perfect for a quick and easy lunch or dinner. Avocados compliment the nutritious coconut perfectly, packed with heart-healthy monosaturated fatty acids, potassium and fibre.

Serves 4

100ml coconut milk
Juice and zest of 1 lime
A small handful of coriander
   stalks, finely chopped
190g raw king prawns
Sea salt
Pinch of chilli flakes
2 teaspoons coconut oil
4 small corn tortillas

To serve

1 ripe avocado, finely sliced
2 spring onions, finely sliced
A small handful of coriander
   leaves, roughly chopped
Tabasco chipotle sauce
   (optional)

1. First make the dressing. Whisk the coconut milk to smooth out any lumps. Stir in the lime juice and chopped coriander stalks and set aside.

2. Toss the prawns with a pinch of salt, the chilli flakes and lime zest in a non-metallic bowl. Heat a non-stick frying pan until hot and add the coconut oil. Tip in the prawns and stir-fry for 1–2 minutes, turning occasionally, until opaque and golden. Remove the prawns from the pan using a slotted spoon and set aside.

3. Wipe the pan clean with a piece of kitchen paper then heat the tortillas in the pan for about 10 seconds to warm through and soften.

4. Take a tortilla and scatter over a portion of the avocado and spring onion, followed by the prawns. Sprinkle over the coriander leaves, spoon over the dressing and top with a dash of Tabasco, if using. Wrap up and serve immediately.

CHICKEN SOUP WITH BABY CORN & LIME

*DAIRY-FREE

This delicately spiced, fragrant soup makes a wonderful meal all year round. It is traditionally fairly spicy – feel free to adjust the chilli content according to taste.

Serves 4

1 tablespoon coconut oil

5cm piece of fresh ginger, peeled and roughly sliced

4 shallots, peeled and halved

4 kaffir lime leaves, or zest of 2 limes

1–2 green chillies (depending on heat preference), halved lengthways

2 lemongrass stalks, bruised with the back of a knife

2 whole chicken legs, skin on

1.2 litres good-quality chicken stock

400ml can coconut milk

2 teaspoons coconut or palm sugar

150g baby corn, roughly sliced

200g button or shiitake mushrooms, sliced

1½ tablespoons fish sauce

Juice of 1 lime, plus extra wedges to serve

A handful of coriander, roughly chopped

1. Heat the oil in a large saucepan over a medium heat. Add the ginger, shallots, lime leaves or zest, chillies and lemongrass and fry for 2–3 minutes, until everything has a bit of colour.

2. Add the chicken and continue to fry for a further 3-4 minutes, until the chicken is light golden. Pour in the stock and bring the mixture up to a boil. Reduce the heat and simmer for 20–25 minutes, until the chicken juices run completely clear. Remove the chicken from the pan and set aside to cool slightly, before stripping the meat from the bone, tearing it into bite-sized pieces.

3. Strain the cooking liquid into another large saucepan, pressing everything down in the sieve to extract as much flavour as possible. Add the coconut milk to the pan, along with the sugar. Heat the soup until simmering, then add the corn and mushrooms and cook for a further 2 minutes. Return the chicken to the pan to warm through. Stir in the fish sauce and lime juice.

4. Ladle the soup into individual bowls and serve sprinkled with coriander and a wedge of lime.

CREAMY RED LENTIL & COCONUT DAHL

*VEGETARIAN *DAIRY-FREE *GLUTEN-FREE

This uses a few spices, but once you've bought them, this dish becomes a wonderful store-cupboard supper. Garlic is a great source of vitamin C and manganese, as well as minerals including calcium and potassium. Ginger is great for blood circulation and has been used for generations as an anti-inflammatory and cure for nausea.

Serves 4

1 tablespoon coconut oil
2 garlic cloves, crushed
2.5cm piece of fresh ginger, peeled and finely grated
1 green chilli, finely chopped
1 teaspoon white mustard seeds
½ teaspoon nigella seeds
1 teaspoon cumin seeds
1 onion, finely sliced
½ teaspoon ground turmeric
200g red lentils
400g can chopped tomatoes
400ml can coconut milk
Sea salt and freshly ground black pepper

To serve
A handful of coriander leaves
Natural yogurt (optional)

1. Heat the oil in a large frying pan over a low to medium heat. Add the garlic, ginger and chilli and fry for a minute or so, until fragrant. Add all of the seeds and fry for a further minute, until the spices smell slightly toasted and aromatic. Scrape in the onion and fry for a further 5–6 minutes, until softened. Stir through the turmeric and fry for a final minute, before adding the lentils.

2. Tip in the tomatoes and coconut milk and season to taste. Half-fill the tomato can with water and add to the pan. Bring the mixture up to a boil and reduce the heat to a simmer. Allow the dahl to gently bubble away, stirring from time to time, for 20–25 minutes, until the lentils are tender and the sauce has thickened and reduced.

3. Divide the dahl between four bowls and serve with a sprinkle of coriander and dollop of yogurt. It also goes very well with the Seeded Coconut Flour Bread on page 60.

CAULIFLOWER & GARLIC SOUP

*VEGETARIAN *DAIRY-FREE

Roasting cauliflower and garlic brings out their natural nuttiness and sweetness. This soup is simplicity at its best – few ingredients brought together by the soothing creaminess of coconut milk.

Serves 4

1 garlic bulb, sliced
  widthways across the
  middle
2 tablespoons coconut oil,
  melted
800g cauliflower, cut into
  florets
1 onion, sliced
Sea salt and freshly ground
  black pepper
250ml coconut milk
750ml good-quality
  vegetable stock

To serve
A handful of parsley,
  roughly chopped

1. Preheat the oven to 200°C/fan 180°C/gas mark 6. Drizzle each half of garlic with a little of the coconut oil and wrap them in foil. Place on a baking tray and roast in the oven for 20 minutes.

2. Place the cauliflower and onion in another baking tray and pour over the remaining oil. Season lightly and give everything a good stir. Transfer to the oven and roast for 20–25 minutes, until golden and just tender. Remove both trays from the oven. By now the garlic should be golden and completely soft.

3. Tip the cauliflower and onion into a food-processor. Squeeze the garlic out of its papery skin and add to the processor, along with the coconut milk. Whizz until smooth, then transfer to a saucepan. Add the stock and heat until just simmering. Taste and check the seasoning.

4. Divide the soup between individual bowls and sprinkle with the parsley.

PEACH & VANILLA
CHIA PUDDINGS

*VEGETARIAN *DAIRY-FREE *GLUTEN-FREE

Nutrient-packed chia seeds are bolstered by the good fats in coconut milk – a winning combination. These 'puddings' also make a great light breakfast before exercise. Peaches work brilliantly, but the puddings will taste delicious with any fruit.

Serves 2

40g chia seeds
200ml coconut milk
200ml almond milk
Seeds from 1 vanilla pod

To serve

1 ripe peach, stoned and
  sliced
A small handful of pistachios
  (about 20g), roughly
  chopped

1. Place the chia seeds in a jug or bowl and pour over the milks and vanilla seeds. Stir until everything is well dispersed, then divide the mixture between two bowls or jars. Chill in the fridge for at least 2 hours or overnight.

2. To serve, top each pudding with the sliced peach and sprinkle with pistachios.

To get the seeds from a vanilla pod, split it in half lengthways with a knife, then scrape the seeds out with the blunt edge of the knife.

COCONUT CREAMS & GRILLED PINEAPPLE

*DAIRY-FREE *GLUTEN-FREE

These little desserts capture the pure essence of coconut. The rich, creamy sweetness is complemented perfectly by the slight tartness of the pineapple. They're easy enough to make midweek for yourself but impressive enough to serve to dinner guests.

Serves 4

4 gelatine leaves
600ml coconut milk
50g coconut sugar
1 vanilla pod, split in half,
   seeds scraped out with
   a knife
A few gratings of nutmeg
½ pineapple, cut lengthways
   into eight wedges

1. Drop the gelatine leaves into a bowl of cold water and push down to submerge. Set aside to soak for 5 minutes.

2. In a saucepan, gently heat the coconut milk with the coconut sugar, vanilla pod and seeds and nutmeg until barely simmering. Remove the vanilla pod from the pan and discard.

3. Lift the softened gelatine from the water and stir into the coconut milk mixture until completely dissolved. Pour into four glasses or ramekins and refrigerate for a minimum of 2 hours to set.

4. Preheat a griddle pan over a medium heat. Cook the pineapple wedges for 2 minutes per side, until lightly caramelised. Set aside to cool slightly.

5. Divide between individual plates and serve alongside the creams.

INSTANT ICE CREAM
*VEGETARIAN *DAIRY-FREE *GLUTEN-FREE

This ice cream really is a kind of magic. Frozen fruit and coconut milk is processed until it whips up into a light, fluffy ice cream. It is best eaten straight away, but can be frozen once made.

Serves 4

4 large ripe bananas,
   roughly sliced and frozen
   for at least 8 hours
200ml coconut milk,
   poured into a freezer bag
   or ice cube tray and frozen
   for at least 8 hours

To serve
Pinch of cinnamon
Coconut chips

1. Remove the banana and coconut milk from the freezer and place in a food-processer. Blitz for 3-4 minutes, until the mixture is completely smooth and has whipped to a light, ice cream consistency.

2. Serve immediately, sprinkled with a little cinnamon and some coconut chips.

If you choose to freeze the ice cream once it has been made, simply set aside at room temperature for 10–15 minutes before serving.

OIL

NUTTY GRANOLA

*VEGETARIAN *DAIRY-FREE

Making your own granola is not just cheaper but far
more delicious than anything shop-bought. Double the
benefit by serving with coconut yogurt or coconut milk.
Or scatter it over your favourite smoothie (try the ones
on pages 14 and 20).

Makes 12–16 servings

500g rolled oats
4 tablespoons coconut oil,
   melted
4 tablespoons maple syrup
1 teaspoon vanilla extract
100g mixed seeds
   (e.g. pumpkin, sunflower
   and chia)
150g mixed nuts (cashews,
   almonds and pecans work
   well), roughly chopped
100g dried berries
   (e.g. cherries, cranberries
   and blueberries)

1. Preheat the oven to 170°C/
fan 150°C/gas mark 3. Place the
oats in a large mixing bowl and
drizzle over the oil, maple syrup
and vanilla. Add the seeds and
nuts and give the mixture a good
stir.

2. Sprinkle the granola into two
lined baking trays and cook for
15–20 minutes, until crisp and
golden.

3. Allow the granola to cool
before stirring through the
berries. Transfer to an airtight
container and keep for up to a
month.

BEETROOT & HORSERADISH SOUP

*VEGETARIAN

This warming, seasonal soup is perfect for a wintry lunch. The beetroot is full of antioxidants and is bolstered by the vitamin C and zinc in the horseradish – great for keeping winter colds at bay. Either serve the horseradish swirled into the soup or in a separate bowl so everyone can have as much or as little as they like.

Serves 4

1 tablespoon coconut oil
1 onion, finely chopped
1kg beetroot, peeled and
 roughly chopped
A few sprigs of thyme
1 litre good-quality
 vegetable stock
Sea salt and freshly ground
 black pepper

To serve

125ml soured cream or yogurt
2 teaspoons grated
 horseradish
A handful of parsley,
 roughly chopped

1. Heat the oil in a large saucepan over a low to medium heat. Add the onion and cook, stirring occasionally, for 5–6 minutes, until softened. Tip in the beetroot and continue to fry for a further 2–3 minutes. Add the thyme to the pan, pour in the stock and simmer for 25–30 minutes, until the beetroot is tender.

2. In a food-processor or blender, whizz the mixture until smooth. Return the soup to the pan and reheat slightly. Season to taste.

3. Divide the soup into individual bowls. Whisk the soured cream or yogurt with the horseradish until smooth and swirl into the soup. Sprinkle with the parsley.

If you can't find it fresh, it's perfectly fine to use horseradish from a jar, but choose grated, hot horseradish rather than cream.

SWEET POTATO & HARISSA SOUP

*VEGETARIAN *DAIRY-FREE

Sweet potatoes work brilliantly with rich, creamy coconut and earthy spices in this silky and satisfying soup. The soup also freezes brilliantly.

Serves 4

1 tablespoon coconut oil
1 onion, finely chopped
1 teaspoon ground cumin
800g sweet potatoes, peeled and finely chopped
1 litre good-quality vegetable stock
250ml coconut milk
Sea salt and freshly ground black pepper

To serve
2 teaspoons good-quality harissa paste
Pinch of chilli flakes

1. Heat the oil in a large saucepan over a low to medium heat. Add the onion and cook, stirring occasionally, for 5–6 minutes, until softened. Add the cumin and fry for a further minute, until you can smell the spices. Tip in the sweet potato and fry for a minute or so, until the potato is slightly golden.

2. Pour in the stock and coconut milk and simmer for 15–20 minutes, until the sweet potato is tender. Tip the soup into a food-processor and whizz until smooth. Season to taste.

3. Serve in individual bowls with a swirl of harissa and the chilli flakes.

This soup goes really well with the Herbed Flatbreads on page 63.

BAKED MEXICAN EGGS *VEGETARIAN *DAIRY-FREE *GLUTEN-FREE

These richly savoury eggs make a deeply satisfying brunch. If you want to get ahead, simply make up the tomato sauce the day before and reheat before dropping in the eggs.

Serves 2

2 teaspoons coconut oil
1 red onion, finely sliced
2 garlic cloves, crushed
1 red pepper, finely sliced
½ red chilli, finely chopped
400g can chopped tomatoes
Sea salt and freshly ground
   black pepper
100g kale leaves (tough stems
   removed), finely chopped
4 medium eggs

To serve
A handful of coriander

1. Preheat the oven to 200°C/fan 180°C/gas mark 6. Heat the oil in a medium-sized, oven-proof frying pan over a low to medium heat. Add the onion and fry for 6–8 minutes, until softened. If the onions are starting to catch during cooking, add a splash of water.

2. Add the garlic, peppers and chilli to the pan and fry for 2–3 minutes, until the garlic is fragrant and the peppers start to take on a little colour. Pour in the chopped tomatoes and simmer for 5 minutes, until the sauce has reduced slightly and the peppers are tender. Season lightly.

3. Stir through the kale and make four wells in the sauce. Crack an egg into each well and transfer to the oven for 4–5 minutes, or until the eggs are cooked to your liking. To serve, sprinkle over the coriander, put it on the table and tuck in.

MUSHROOM, FETA & SPINACH OMELETTE

*VEGETARIAN *GLUTEN-FREE

This omelette is wonderfully simple to prepare and the protein in the eggs and feta will keep you satisfied for hours. Eggs and mushrooms are also high in selenium and vitamin D.

Makes 2

3 teaspoons coconut oil
1 garlic clove, finely sliced
100g chestnut mushrooms,
    sliced
50g feta cheese, crumbled
4 medium eggs, beaten
Sea salt and freshly ground
    black pepper

To serve
A large handful of baby
    spinach leaves
Lemon juice

1. Heat a teaspoon of oil in a medium, non-stick frying pan over a medium heat. Add the garlic and fry for a few minutes. Then add the mushrooms and fry for a further 2–3 minutes, turning occasionally, until golden. Remove from the pan with a slotted spoon and transfer to a bowl. Mix the mushrooms with the feta cheese and set aside.

2. Return the pan to the heat and add another teaspoon of the oil. Reduce the heat slightly, season the beaten egg with a pinch of salt and pepper and pour in half of the beaten egg. Swirl the egg around the pan and mix with a spatula, until the omelette begins to set. Once the egg is almost set (this should take

about 2 minutes), sprinkle half the mushroom and feta mix onto one side of the omelette and top with the spinach and a squeeze of lemon. Carefully fold the other half over and slide onto a plate.

3. Repeat with the remaining egg to make a second omelette and serve on individual plates.

PAPRIKA & LIME SWEET POTATO WEDGES

*VEGETARIAN *DAIRY-FREE *GLUTEN-FREE

A light and smoky take on traditional chips, these wedges are delicious simply served with a spicy mayonnaise or as a side dish, plus they're packed with vitamin A for healthy skin. They pair brilliantly with the Turkey Burgers on page 57.

Serves 4

600g sweet potatoes,
  scrubbed and each potato
  cut into eight wedges
Zest of 2 limes
Sea salt and freshly
  ground black pepper
1½ teaspoons sweet
  smoked paprika
1½ tablespoons coconut
  oil, melted
4 tablespoons good-quality
  mayonnaise
Tabasco

1. Preheat the oven to 200°C/fan 180°C/gas mark 6. Place the sweet potato wedges in a large bowl and sprinkle over the zest of one lime, a pinch of salt and pepper and the paprika. Drizzle over the oil and toss the wedges until well coated.

2. Lay the wedges out in a single layer on a baking tray and cook for 20–25 minutes, turning halfway through until crisp and golden.

3. Mix the mayonnaise with the remaining lime zest and a few drops of Tabasco and serve with the potato wedges.

SLOW-ROASTED TOMATO SAUCE

*VEGETARIAN *DAIRY-FREE *GLUTEN-FREE

Roasting tomatoes slowly brings out their natural sweetness beautifully. This rustic sauce is delicious as it is, paired with any pasta of your choice, or blitzed to make a finer sauce.

Serves 6–8

1kg ripe or overripe
  tomatoes, halved
1 small onion, chopped
4 fat garlic cloves, finely
  chopped
2 tablespoons coconut oil,
  melted
Pinch of sugar
Sea salt and freshly ground
  black pepper

To serve
A handful of basil leaves

1. Preheat the oven to 180°C/ fan 160°C/gas mark 4. Lay the tomatoes, cut-side up, on one or two baking trays in a single layer. Scatter over the onions and dot each tomato with a little of the chopped garlic. Drizzle over the oil and season with the sugar, salt and pepper.

2. Roast in the oven for 50–60 minutes, until the tomatoes are completely soft and the skins slightly burnished.

3. The tomatoes can be left whole and run through a pasta of your choice, with the basil leaves scattered over, or blitzed to make a chunky sauce.

The roasted tomatoes can be kept halved or blitzed for up to a week in the fridge, covered.

PEARL BARLEY & SQUASH RISOTTO

*VEGETARIAN *DAIRY-FREE

Pearl barley offers a wholesome and nutritious alternative to rice in this delicate risotto. It has a far higher percentage of fibre than brown and white rice, which aids good digestion.

Serves 4

3 teaspoons coconut oil
1 small butternut squash, (700–800g), peeled and cut into 1–2cm cubes
2 shallots, peeled and finely chopped
2 garlic cloves, crushed
A small handful of sage leaves, roughly chopped (reserve a little for garnish)
300g pearl barley
1.5 litres good-quality vegetable stock
Juice of ½ lemon

To serve

Sea salt and freshly ground black pepper
A handful of parsley, finely chopped

1. Heat 2 teaspoons of the oil in a large frying pan over a medium heat. Add the squash and fry for 3–4 minutes, turning from time to time, until golden. Remove from the pan and set aside.

2. Add the remaining oil to the pan, reduce the heat and scrape in the shallots. Fry for 4–5 minutes, until softened. Add the garlic, half the sage and continue to fry for a further minute, until the garlic is fragrant.

3. Pour the pearl barley into the pan and stir for 1–2 minutes, to toast the barley slightly. Add a ladle of stock, stirring occasionally, until the liquid is absorbed. Continue to add the stock like this and keep stirring, then add the lemon juice.

4. Stir the squash back into the risotto after 15 minutes and cook for a further 15 minutes or so, until the barley is tender and you have used up all the stock.

5. Divide the risotto between individual plates, top with the remaining sage, parsley and a pinch of salt and pepper.

PRAWNS WITH ASIAN GREENS & NOODLES

*DAIRY-FREE *GLUTEN-FREE

This flavoursome, nutritious stir-fry can be thrown together in less than 30 minutes – ideal for a light midweek dinner.

Serves 4

200g brown rice noodles
1 tablespoon coconut oil
2cm piece of fresh ginger, peeled and finely grated
2 garlic cloves, crushed
2 pak choi, stems and leaves roughly sliced
150g sugar snap peas, halved
180g raw tiger prawns, de-veined if necessary

For the sauce

2 tablespoons tamari
2 teaspoons coconut or palm sugar
Juice of 1 lime
1 red chilli, finely chopped

To serve

2 spring onions, finely chopped
1 tablespoon sesame seeds, toasted

1. Start by soaking the noodles in a bowl of boiling water for 5 minutes, until almost tender. Drain, rinse under cold water and set aside.

2. Now make the sauce. Stir together the tamari, sugar, lime juice and chilli and set aside.

3. Heat the oil in a large frying pan or wok over a medium heat. Throw in the ginger and garlic, stir-fry for a minute or so and then stir in the pak choi stems and sugar snap peas. Stir fry for a minute, then add the prawns, frying for a further minute before pouring over the sauce. Allow the sauce to bubble for a minute or so, until the prawns are opaque and the sauce has reduced slightly.

4. Add the pak choi leaves and stir for a minute until they start to wilt slightly. Toss the noodles in the pan to reheat, mixing everything together, then divide between individual plates or bowls, scattered with the spring onions and sesame seeds.

MISO SALMON &
AUBERGINE SKEWERS
*DAIRY-FREE

These skewers are so simple to prepare and yet incredibly delicious. The white miso caramelises under the grill to a perfectly balanced savoury sweetness that all the family will love.

Serves 4

For the marinade
50g white miso paste
2 teaspoons coconut oil, melted
2 tablespoons mirin
1 tablespoon tamari soy sauce
2.5cm piece of fresh ginger, peeled and finely grated

For the skewers
1 aubergine, cut in half lengthways, each half cut into eight chunks
4 salmon fillets, skinned and cut in half horizontally

To serve
1 tablespoon sesame seeds
2 spring onions, finely sliced
A handful of fresh herbs (coriander works well)

1. First make the marinade. Spoon the miso paste into a bowl and whisk in the coconut oil, mirin, tamari and ginger.

2. Next add the aubergine and salmon to the bowl and stir well until thoroughly coated in the marinade. Set aside in the fridge for up to an hour or cook immediately.

3. Preheat the grill to high. Thread one chunk of aubergine followed by a piece of salmon and then another chunk of aubergine onto each skewer. Transfer the skewers to a foil-lined baking tray.

4. Grill the skewers for 1–2 minutes each side, until the fish is cooked through and everything is nicely caramelised.

5. Divide the skewers amongst four plates and scatter with the sesame seeds, spring onions and herbs.

VEGAN CHILLI WITH GUACAMOLE & SALSA

Vegan chilli can be just as tasty and nutritious as its meaty counterpart – rich, earthy spices, delicate sweet potatoes and creamy beans, finished with spicy guacamole and salsa, create a wonderfully balanced meal.

Serves 4–6

For the chilli

3 teaspoons coconut oil
600g sweet potatoes, scrubbed and cut into 2cm cubes
1 teaspoon ground cumin
1 teaspoon mild chilli powder
1 teaspoon smoked paprika
1 onion, finely chopped
2 garlic cloves, crushed
1 green pepper, chopped
2 × 400g cans chopped tomatoes
1 tablespoon tomato purée
400g can kidney beans
400g can black beans
Sea salt and freshly ground black pepper

cont. overleaf

1. First make the chilli. Heat 1 teaspoon of the oil in a large frying pan over a medium heat. Tip in the sweet potato chunks and fry for 4-5 minutes, until nicely golden on all sides. Remove from the pan with a slotted spoon and set aside.

2. Reduce the heat slightly and add the remaining oil. Once melted, add the spices. Fry for 1-2 minutes, until aromatic.

3. Reduce the heat again, add the onion and fry very gently, stirring from time to time, for 5-6 minutes, until softened. Stir in the garlic and green pepper and continue to fry for a further 2-3 minutes, until the pepper has taken on a little colour and the garlic has softened.

4. Add the chopped tomatoes and purée, tip the sweet potato back into the pan, turn the heat up a little and simmer for 6-8 minutes, until the mixture has slightly reduced and thickened. Drain and rinse the kidney and black beans, add to the pan and simmer for a further 5 minutes, seasoning to taste. By now, the mixture should be fairly thick and the sweet potato tender.

cont. overleaf

VEGAN CHILLI WITH GUACAMOLE & SALSA
CONT.

For the guacamole

1 large ripe avocado
½ shallot, finely chopped
½ red chilli, finely diced
Juice of ½ lime (reserve half
   for the salsa)
1–2 tablespoons roughly
   chopped coriander leaves

For the salsa

150g cherry tomatoes,
   quartered
½ shallot, finely chopped
½ red chilli, finely diced
Lime juice
1–2 tablespoons roughly
   chopped coriander leaves

5. Now make the guacamole.
Scoop the avocado flesh into
a bowl and add the shallot,
chilli, half the lime juice and the
coriander. Mash the mixture with
a fork and season with a little salt.

6. For the salsa, place the
tomatoes in a separate bowl
and add the remaining shallot,
chilli, lime juice and coriander.
Season to taste with salt and stir
to combine.

7. Divide the chilli into individual
bowls and serve with a dollop of
the guacamole and salsa.

GRIDDLED CHICKEN
WITH GREEK SALAD
*GLUTEN-FREE

This Greek-inspired dish is reminiscent of warm summer holiday evenings. While delicious served warm, the chicken can be cooked in advance and eaten cold with the salad. The onion, vinegar and tomatoes add an antioxidant boost.

Serves 4

4 medium chicken breasts, skinned
Juice and zest of 1 lemon
A small handful of fresh oregano, finely chopped, or ½ teaspoon dried
Sea salt and freshly ground black pepper
2 teaspoons coconut oil, melted

For the salad

1 red onion, finely sliced
1 tablespoon white wine or cider vinegar
200g ripe vine tomatoes
50g black Kalamata olives, pitted
1 cucumber, peeled, deseeded and roughly sliced
80g good-quality feta cheese, crumbled
2 teaspoons fresh oregano, roughly chopped, or 1 teaspoon dried

1. Lay the chicken breasts between two sheets of greaseproof paper and beat with a rolling pin to flatten the meat out slightly.

2. Place the chicken in a bowl and pour over the lemon juice and zest and oregano and season with salt and pepper. Marinate the chicken for at least an hour, or preferably overnight in the fridge.

3. Remove the chicken from the fridge 15 minutes before you're ready to cook it. Heat a griddle pan over a medium heat. Drizzle the coconut oil over the chicken and, once the pan is fairly hot, cook the chicken for 4–5 minutes on each side, until the chicken juices run clear.

4. Now make the salad. Put the onion in a salad bowl and pour over the vinegar. Add the tomatoes, olives, cucumber and feta.

5. Divide the chicken amongst four plates, sprinkle over the oregano and serve with the salad.

TURKEY BURGERS
& FENNEL SLAW
GLUTEN-FREE

These quick and flavoursome burgers are great for a quick midweek supper or a summer barbecue. The crisp and citrusy salad makes a delicious alternative to creamy coleslaw.

Serves 4

For the burgers

500g turkey mince

3 spring onions, finely sliced

50g sharp cheese (e.g. feta or Lancashire), crumbled

2 tablespoons parsley, finely chopped

Sea salt and freshly ground black pepper

2 teaspoons coconut oil

For the slaw

1 large fennel bulb, finely sliced

1 shallot, finely sliced

¼ red cabbage, finely sliced

1 orange, peeled and segmented

½ teaspoon fennel seeds

2 teaspoons olive oil

20g pecans, roughly chopped

1. First make the burgers. Combine the mince with the spring onions, cheese and parsley, then season with salt and pepper. Shape the mixture into four patties and set aside.

2. Heat the oil in a large, non-stick frying pan over a medium heat. Add the burgers and fry for 5–6 minutes on each side, until golden and completely cooked through.

3. To make the slaw, mix all the ingredients together and season with a little salt and pepper.

4. Divide the burgers amongst four plates and serve with the fennel slaw.

Choose turkey thigh mince as it is more flavoursome and juicy than breast. It's also leaner than chicken.

FLOUR

SEEDED COCONUT FLOUR BREAD

*VEGETARIAN *GLUTEN-FREE *DAIRY-FREE

This richly seeded bread doesn't require any kneading or proving – just mix and bake. It's also a great gluten- and dairy-free staple. It's wonderful either simply sliced or toasted with nut butter.

Makes a 2lb loaf

150g ground almonds
100g coconut flour
1½ teaspoons baking powder
½ teaspoon bicarbonate of soda
Sea salt
75g mixed seeds (e.g. poppy seeds, sunflower seeds, linseeds and sunflower seeds)
6 large eggs
50g coconut oil, melted
1½ tablespoons lemon juice

1. Preheat the oven to 190°C/fan 170°C/gas mark 5. Place the ground almonds in a large mixing bowl, breaking up any lumps as you go. Sift over the coconut flour, baking powder and bicarbonate of soda, stir through the salt and seeds and make a well in the centre.

2. Beat in the eggs, coconut oil and lemon juice and transfer to a 2lb loaf tin lined with greaseproof paper. Bake for 40–45 minutes, until golden and cooked through.

3. Allow the bread to cool in the tin for 10 minutes, then transfer it to a wire rack to cool completely. The bread will keep in an airtight container for up to 3 days.

STICKY DATE LOAF

*VEGETARIAN *GLUTEN-FREE *DAIRY-FREE

A healthier take on traditional sticky toffee pudding, this loaf is equally delicious and full of fibre and protein to boot. Enjoy warm with a generous helping of 'toffee' sauce.

Serves 12

200g Medjool dates, pitted and finely chopped
250ml boiling water
1 teaspoon bicarbonate of soda
60g coconut oil, melted
50g coconut sugar
3 large eggs, lightly beaten
1 teaspoon vanilla extract
125g gluten-free plain flour
75g coconut flour
1 teaspoon baking powder
1 teaspoon xanthum gum

For the sauce
150ml coconut cream
30g coconut sugar
1 teaspoon vanilla extract

1. Preheat the oven to 180°C/ fan 160°C/gas mark 4. Lightly grease a 2lb loaf tin and line with greaseproof paper.

2. Place the chopped dates in a bowl, pour over the boiling water and stir through the bicarbonate of soda. Set aside until needed.

3. In a separate, large mixing bowl, beat the oil, sugar, eggs and vanilla together until smooth. Sift over the flours, baking powder and xanthum gum and fold through until you have a thick batter. Add the dates, along with their soaking water, and fold through to loosen the mixture.

4. Pour into the prepared tin and bake for 45–50 minutes, until risen and golden. A skewer inserted into the centre should come out clean.

5. Remove the cake from the oven and allow to cool in the tin for 10 minutes before turning out.

6. Next make the sauce. Pour the coconut cream and sugar into a saucepan, place over a medium heat and simmer for 5–6 minutes, until slightly thickened. Stir through the vanilla and serve with a slice of the loaf. The cake is best served warm but will keep in an airtight container for up to 3 days.

Check the cake after 30 minutes – if it's looking a little dark, cover it with a piece of foil and return it to the oven.

HERBED FLATBREADS

*VEGETARIAN *GLUTEN-FREE *DAIRY-FREE

These simple flatbreads are so easy to make and a perfect vehicle for dips, dahls and soups. Try them with the Sweet Potato & Harissa Soup on page 39.

Makes 4

50g coconut flour
½ teaspoon xantham gum
1 teaspoon baking powder
Sea salt
3 medium eggs, beaten
2 tablespoons mixed fresh
  herbs (e.g. parsley, thyme,
  rosemary and sage),
  finely chopped
2 tablespoons coconut oil,
  melted

1. Sift the flour, xantham gum, baking powder and a good pinch of salt into a bowl.

2. Make a well in the centre and add the egg, herbs and coconut oil. Gradually beat the wet ingredients into the dry ones to create a thick batter.

3. Heat a non-stick frying pan over a medium heat. With damp hands, shape a quarter of the mixture into a flatbread or pitta shape. Place in the pan and dry-fry for 2–3 minutes per side or until golden brown. Repeat until you have made four flatbreads.

SMOKEY SWEETCORN FRITTERS
*VEGETARIAN *GLUTEN-FREE *DAIRY-FREE

Smokey, sweet and nutritious fritters make a wonderful brunch-time treat, full of vitamins, minerals and antioxidants from the avocado and tomato.

Serves 4

For the fritters

400g sweetcorn (drained weight)
40g coconut flour
25g gluten-free flour
1½ teaspoons baking powder
¼ teaspoon sea salt
1 teaspoon smoked paprika
2 spring onions, finely chopped
1 red chilli, finely chopped
3 medium eggs, lightly beaten
100–150ml almond milk
2 teaspoons coconut oil

For the salsa

100g tomatoes, roughly chopped
1 shallot, finely chopped
A handful of fresh parsley and coriander, roughly chopped
Juice of 1 lime
1 large ripe avocado, stoned, peeled and finely sliced

1. Place 300g of the sweetcorn in a mixing bowl and sift over the flours, baking powder, salt and paprika. Add the spring onion and chilli to the bowl and stir everything to combine.

2. Pour the remaining sweetcorn into a food-processor, add the eggs and whizz until the mixture is fairly smooth. Pour this over the sweetcorn and flour and beat until the mixture forms a batter. Add the almond milk, a little at a time, to achieve a fairly thick, pourable consistency.

3. Heat the oil in a non-stick frying pan over a medium heat and drop 2 heaped tablespoons of the batter into the pan. Fry for 2–3 minutes on each side, until

golden and cooked through. Repeat with the remaining batter. Set aside and keep warm.

4. To make the salsa, mix the tomatoes, shallot, herbs and lime together and pour over the avocado.

5. Serve a stack of pancakes on a big plate, topped with the salsa, and tuck in.

PEANUT BUTTER COOKIES *VEGETARIAN *GLUTEN-FREE

These nutty cookies are perfect for an afternoon treat. They tend to rise quite a bit during cooking so patting them into discs will help to retain a cookie-like shape.

Makes 16–20

75g ground almonds
60g coconut flour
1 teaspoon baking powder
1 teaspoon xanthum gum
150g crunchy peanut butter
75g coconut oil, melted
3 medium eggs, beaten
75g coconut sugar
50ml maple syrup
1 teaspoon vanilla extract
50g good-quality dark
  chocolate, minimum
  70 per cent cocoa solids,
  finely chopped

1. Preheat the oven to 180°C/ fan 160°C/gas mark 4. Line two baking trays with greaseproof paper

2. Sprinkle the ground almonds into a large mixing bowl, breaking up any lumps as you go. Sift over the coconut flour, baking powder and xanthum gum. Now make a well in the centre.

3. Place the peanut butter into the well, then add the oil, eggs, sugar, maple syrup and vanilla. Beat the wet ingredients into the dry to create a thick batter. Stir in the chocolate.

4. Pat tablespoons of the mixture into discs using your palms, then transfer to the prepared trays, leaving a gap of at least 2cm between each disc.

5. Bake the cookies for 10–12 minutes, until risen and golden. Allow the cookies to cool on the trays for 10 minutes before transferring to a cooling rack. The cookies are delicious warm but will keep in an airtight container for up to 3 days.

PANCAKES WITH MAPLE BANANAS

*VEGETARIAN *GLUTEN-FREE *DAIRY-FREE

Once you've tried these fluffy pancakes with rich, caramelised bananas they are sure to become a breakfast or brunch staple. Coconut flour produces a far lighter pancake than its stodgy, glutinous counterpart.

Serves 2

50g coconut flour
1 teaspoon baking powder
Sea salt
3 tablespoons coconut oil, melted, plus a little extra for frying
4 large eggs, lightly beaten
100ml coconut or almond milk
2 bananas, sliced
6 tablespoons maple syrup

1. First make the batter. Sift the flour and baking powder into a mixing bowl. Stir in the salt and make a well in the centre of the flour. Pour in the oil and eggs and whisk to gradually incorporate the flour. Whisk in enough milk to achieve a double cream consistency.

2. Heat a little coconut oil in a large, non-stick frying pan and drop 2 tablespoons of the batter into rounds, leaving a little space between each. Fry the pancakes for 1–2 minutes. When the edges are set and there are bubbles covering the surface of the pancakes flip them over and continue to cook for a further 1–2 minutes until risen, golden and fluffy. Set aside and keep warm while you repeat the process until the batter has been used up.

3. Keep the pan on the heat and add a little more oil. Tip in the sliced bananas and fry for 30 seconds, until they start to take on a little colour. Pour in 2 tablespoons of the maple syrup, turn the bananas over and fry for a further 30–60 seconds, until golden and syrupy.

4. Divide the pancakes between two plates and serve with the bananas and remaining maple syrup.

ORANGE & POPPY SEED MUFFINS

*VEGETARIAN *DAIRY-FREE

These fibre and protein-rich muffins are an excellent breakfast or teatime treat. When in season, try using sweet, ruby fleshed blood oranges for variety.

Makes 12

200g spelt flour
50g coconut flour
1 teaspoon baking powder
½ teaspoon bicarbonate
  of soda
4 medium eggs, lightly beaten
75g coconut oil or butter,
  melted
100g coconut sugar
2 oranges, zested, flesh
  peeled and cut into six
  slices each
2 tablespoons poppy seeds
100–150ml almond or
  coconut milk

1. Preheat the oven to 180°C/fan 160°C/gas mark 4. Line a 12-hole muffin tray with paper liners.

2. Sift the flours, baking powder and bicarbonate of soda into a large bowl. Make a hole in the centre of the dry ingredients and pour in the egg, coconut oil or butter, sugar, orange zest and poppy seeds. Use a metal spoon to fold the wet ingredients into the dry, adding in the milk to loosen to a dropping consistency.

3. Fill each muffin case two thirds full and top with a slice of orange. Bake for 18–20 minutes, until a skewer inserted into the centre of each muffin comes out clean.

4. Serve warm or cold. These muffins will keep in an airtight container for up to 2 days.

Using blood oranges gives you an extra boost of vitamin C – they can contain up to 40 per cent more than other oranges.

PISTACHIO BROWNIES

Fudgy chocolate brownies are the last word in indulgence. Try a less sinful treat with this recipe, which is packed with good fats, high-fibre coconut flour and antioxidant-rich dark chocolate.

Makes 16 squares

175g coconut oil or butter
200g good-quality dark
   chocolate, minimum
   70 per cent cocoa solids,
   roughly chopped
50g ground almonds
75g coconut flour
10g cocoa powder
150g coconut sugar
50ml maple syrup
3 medium eggs, lightly beaten
1 teaspoon vanilla extract
100g pistachios, roughly
   chopped

1. Preheat the oven to 180°C/ fan 160°C/gas mark 4. Grease and line a 20cm square tin with greaseproof paper.

2. Add the oil or butter and chocolate to a pan. Melt over a very low heat and allow the mixture to melt, stirring occasionally. As soon as the chocolate and fat has melted, remove from the heat and set aside.

3. Sprinkle the ground almonds into a large mixing bowl, breaking up any lumps as you go. Sift over the coconut flour and cocoa powder.

4. In a separate bowl, beat together the coconut sugar, maple syrup and eggs with an electric whisk until foamy and paler in colour – this will take about 3–4 minutes.

5. Pour the eggy mixture over the dry ingredients and use a large metal spoon to gently fold the mixture through. Pour over the melted chocolate, vanilla extract and three quarters of the pistachios and carefully fold through, so as not to knock out too much air.

6. Place the mixture into the prepared tin, sprinkle over the remaining pistachios and bake for 20–25 minutes, until crisp on top and just set. Allow to cool slightly before cutting into squares. The brownies will keep in an airtight container for up to 3 days.

GRIDDLED VEGETABLES

*VEGETARIAN *GLUTEN-FREE *DAIRY-FREE

Great as a side dish or on their own, these griddled vegetables are matched with a sour kick from the sumac and lemon and tempered by the nutty sweetness of coconut.

Serves 4

For the marinade

2 teaspoons coconut oil, melted
2 garlic cloves, crushed
¼ teaspoon sumac
Zest of 1 lemon (reserve juice, to serve)
Sea salt and freshly ground black pepper

For the vegetables

1 fennel bulb, cut into eight wedges
200g asparagus, woody ends discarded
200g tenderstem broccoli, ends trimmed
200g cherry tomatoes on the vine
20g coconut chips

1. First make the marinade. Pour the coconut oil into a large mixing bowl and add the garlic, sumac and lemon zest. Season with a pinch of salt and pepper, to taste.

2. Tip in the fennel, asparagus, broccoli and tomatoes and toss in the marinade to coat.

3. Place a griddle pan over a medium heat and when hot, lay some of the vegetables on the grill in a single layer. Cook for about 2 minutes on each side, until lightly burnished and tender. Set aside and repeat with the remaining vegetables.

4. Sprinkle the coconut chips over the griddle and toast briefly until golden.

5. Divide the vegetables amongst four individual plates and drizzle with the lemon juice and toasted coconut.

GRILLED COD WITH RADISH & HERBS

*GLUTEN-FREE *DAIRY-FREE

This delicate and vibrant supper requires a keen eye on time but the results are fabulous. The radish salad and coconut chips add a good source of fibre.

Serves 4

4 skinless cod loin fillets,
  weighing about 175g each
2 tablespoons coconut oil,
  melted, or olive oil
Juice and zest of 1 lemon
1 shallot, finely chopped
200g radishes, halved
Sea salt and freshly ground
  black pepper
20g coconut chips

To serve
A handful of mixed fresh
  herbs (e.g. basil, dill and
  parsley), roughly chopped
100g salad leaves

1. Preheat the grill to a medium heat. Brush the fish fillets with half of the oil and place on a baking tray lined with foil. Sprinkle over the lemon zest and grill for 10-12 minutes, until the flesh just flakes to the touch. Set aside and keep warm.

2. Meanwhile, pour the lemon juice over the shallot and set aside. Toss the radishes in the remaining oil, season with a little salt and pepper and grill for 3-4 minutes, until lightly coloured. Sprinkle the coconut chips over the radishes for the final 30 seconds of cooking.

3. Divide the fish amongst four plates and scatter with the shallots, radishes and coconut. Serve the herbs and salad leaves alongside.

SPICY CHICKEN & CUCUMBER SALAD

*GLUTEN-FREE *DAIRY-FREE

The light and nutty crunch of desiccated coconut offers a delicious and high-fibre alternative to breadcrumbed chicken. Serve with a spicy, cooling cucumber salad for a light supper.

Serves 4

60g desiccated coconut

1 lime, zested then cut into wedges for garnish

¼ teaspoon chilli flakes

Sea salt and freshly ground black pepper

1 large egg, lightly beaten

4 medium skinless chicken breasts

1 tablespoon coconut oil, melted

For the salad

1 tablespoon rice wine vinegar

1 teaspoon coconut or palm sugar

1 large cucumber, halved lengthways, deseeded and roughly sliced, or 250g baby cucumbers, sliced

A small handful each of fresh coriander, mint and dill, roughly chopped

1. Preheat the oven to 200°C/ fan 180°C/gas mark 6. Prepare the chicken coating by mixing together in a shallow dish the coconut, lime zest and a pinch of chilli flakes. Season lightly with salt and pepper. Pour the beaten egg into another shallow dish.

2. Dip each chicken breast in the egg, then roll it in the coconut mixture to coat. Transfer to a baking tray, drizzle with the coconut oil and cook for 18–20 minutes, or until the crust is golden and chicken juices run completely clear.

3. Meanwhile, prepare the salad. Mix the vinegar with the sugar until completely dissolved. Toss the cucumber in this dressing and scatter over the herbs and remaining chilli flakes.

4. Divide the chicken and salad amongst individual plates and add a wedge of lime.

PINEAPPLE CARPACCIO

*VEGETARIAN *GLUTEN-FREE *DAIRY-FREE

A carpaccio elevates a simple sliced fruit into something you can show off to guests. The crisp, toasted coconut chips and zingy lime sugar create wonderful textures and flavours.

Serves 4–5

1 fresh pineapple
20g coconut chips
Zest of 1 lime
15g coconut sugar

1. To prepare the pineapple, slice off the base and leaves and stand it upright on a chopping board. Slice off the skin downwards in strips and remove any eyes with a small knife. Lay the pineapple on its side and slice thinly.

2. Toast the coconut chips in a small, non-stick pan until golden. Remove from the heat and set aside.

3. Lay the pineapple slices on a serving dish and sprinkle over the coconut. Mix the lime zest and sugar together, drizzle over the pineapple and serve immediately.

DATE & COCOA ENERGY BALLS

*VEGETARIAN *GLUTEN-FREE *DAIRY-FREE

These delicate energy balls are rather like chocolate truffles, although much better for you – they're full of nutrients and good fats. Enjoy before a gym session or as an afternoon snack.

Makes 16–18

200g Medjool dates, pitted
3 tablespoons cocoa powder
  (check it's dairy-free if
  needed)
1 tablespoon coconut oil
¼ teaspoon cinnamon
60g desiccated coconut, plus
  2 tablespoons to serve

1. Put the dates, oil, cinnamon, coconut and 1 tablespoon of the cocoa powder in a food-processor and blend until fairly smooth.

2. With damp hands, roll the mixture into individual balls. Sprinkle a plate with the remaining coconut and another with the remaining cocoa powder. Roll half the balls in the coconut and half in the cocoa. Refrigerate to set.

These energy balls will keep in the fridge for up to 10 days. They are perfect for snacking when the cravings hit!

OAT & SOUR CHERRY
COOKIES *VEGETARIAN *DAIRY-FREE

Soft and chewy oat cookies jewelled with squidgy
sour cherries go wonderfully with a mug of tea or hot
chocolate (try the Cardamom Hot Chocolate on page 17).
They're also ideal for lunchboxes.

Makes 12–16

40g coconut flour
½ teaspoon baking powder
¼ teaspoon ground cinnamon
90g porridge oats
25g desiccated coconut
75g coconut oil or butter,
   melted
75g coconut or light brown
   soft sugar
50ml maple syrup
1 large egg, lightly beaten
60g dried sour cherries,
   roughly chopped

1. Preheat the oven to 180°C/fan
160°C/gas mark 4. Line two large
baking trays with greaseproof
paper and set aside.

2. Sift the coconut flour, baking
powder and cinnamon into a
large mixing bowl. Stir through
the porridge oats and desiccated
coconut and make a well in the
centre. Pour in the melted oil
or butter, followed by the sugar,
maple syrup and egg. Beat the
wet ingredients into the dry to
make a thick, sticky dough. Stir
through the cherries.

3. Transfer heaped tablespoons of
the mixture onto the baking trays,
leaving a space of at least 4cm
between each one.

4. Bake in the oven for
12–14 minutes, until the biscuits
are golden and risen. Leave to
cool on the trays for 10 minutes
before transferring to a cooling
rack. The cookies will keep in an
airtight tin for up to 3 days.

CRANBERRY & PUMPKIN SEED BARS

*VEGETARIAN *DAIRY-FREE

These oaty bars make an ideal, energy-boosting snack. Rustle up a batch and keep on hand for that mid-afternoon slump.

Makes 12

6 Medjool dates, pitted
50ml hot water
50g coconut oil, melted
2 tablespoons crunchy
   peanut butter
2 tablespoons honey
1 large banana, roughly
   chopped
200g rolled oats
75g desiccated coconut
50g dried cranberries
80g pumpkin seeds

1. Preheat the oven to 160°C/ fan 140°C/gas mark 3. Grease and line a 20cm square tin with greaseproof paper.

2. Soak the dates in the hot water for 10 minutes, to soften. Place them in a food-processor, along with their soaking water, then add the coconut oil, peanut butter, honey and banana. Blend until fairly smooth.

3. Tip the mixture into a bowl and stir in the oats, coconut, cranberries and pumpkin seeds. Spoon into the prepared tin and bake for 50–60 minutes, until golden brown and slightly crisp. Leave to cool before cutting into 12 pieces. The bars will keep in an airtight container for up to 4 days.

For extra depth of flavour, lightly toast the coconut and oats in a dry frying pan before adding to the bar mix.

HEALTHY, SALTED BANOFFEE POTS

*VEGETARIAN *GLUTEN-FREE

These desserts take a little bit of effort but they are well worth it. A healthier version of this classic dessert is a revelation – perfect for entertaining.

Serves 4

For the 'toffee'
200ml coconut cream
50g coconut sugar
Pinch of sea salt

For the base
30g desiccated coconut
30g pecans
1 Medjool date, pitted
1 teaspoon coconut oil

For the topping
125ml coconut cream, chilled
2 bananas, sliced
20g good-quality dark
  chocolate, minimum
  70 per cent cocoa solids,
  grated

1. First make the toffee. Pour the coconut cream and sugar into a small saucepan and place over a medium heat. Bring up to a boil and simmer for 6–8 minutes, stirring frequently, until thickened. Stir in the salt and set aside to cool.

2. When the toffee has cooled to room temperature, transfer it to a bowl, cover with clingfilm and refrigerate for at least 2 hours. It can be made up to a week in advance.

3. For the base, place all the ingredients in a food-processor and blitz until fairly smooth and sticky. Divide the mixture amongst four glasses or ramekins and leave to set in the fridge for an hour.

4. For the topping, whip the coconut cream with an electric whisk until thickened. Then scoop a spoonful of the toffee onto each base and spread it out a little to reach the edges. Scatter over the banana slices, dollop some coconut cream on each one, and sprinkle over the chocolate. Serve immediately.

INDEX

ACKNOWLEDGEMENTS

A big thank you to all at Kyle Books, and in particular Claire Rogers. Thank you to Clare Winfield for the beautiful photography and to Wei for the gorgeous props; it was great to work with such a fun and creative team!

Massive thanks to Nicola for being my right-hand woman and source of much laughter on the shoot days. Also to Poppy for your thorough recipe testing and all-round brilliance.

Enormous thanks to my hugely talented friend, Jenni Desmond, for the wonderful illustrations. I'm so happy that we finally got to work together!

Thank you to my lovely friends, family and Bob for your support, and for being such eager recipe tasters.

For my mum and Jess

First published in Great Britain in 2016 by
Kyle Books, an imprint of Kyle Cathie Ltd
192–198 Vauxhall Bridge Road
London SW1V 1DX
general.enquiries@kylebooks.com
www.kylebooks.co.uk

10 9 8 7 6 5 4 3 2 1

ISBN 978 0 85783 385 3

Project Editor: Claire Rogers
Copy Editor: Eve Pertile
Designer: Helen Bratby
Photographer: Clare Winfield
Illustrator: Jenni Desmond
Food Stylist: Emily Jonzen
Prop Stylist: Wei Tang
Production: Nic Jones and Gemma John

A Cataloguing in Publication record
for this title is available from the British
Library.

Colour reproduction by ALTA London
Printed and bound in China by C&C Offset
Printing Co., Ltd.

* Note: all eggs are free-range

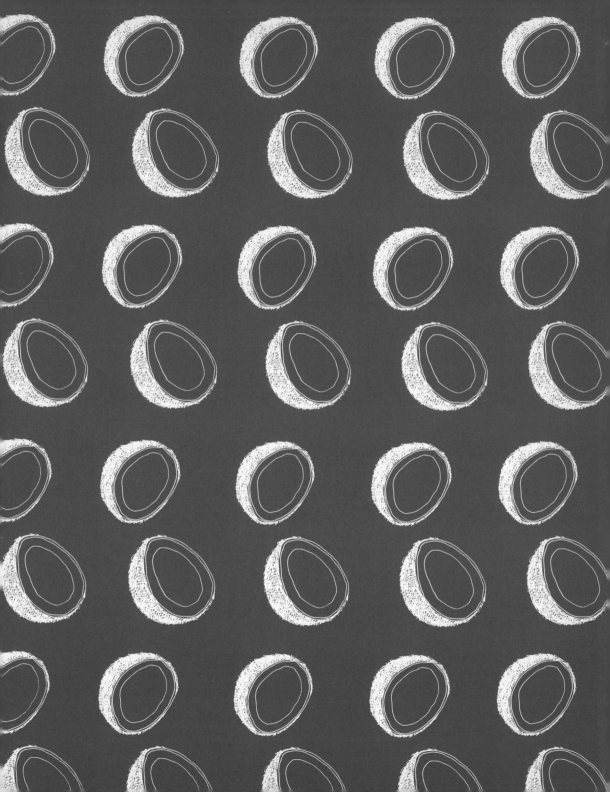